LIFE IN ANCIENT CIVILIZATIONS

The Aztecs
LIFE IN TENOCHTITLAN

by **Matt Doeden**

illustrated by **Samuel Hiti**

M Millbrook Press · Minneapolis

LAKE
TEXCOCO

Tlacopan ● ●Texcoco

Tenochtitlan

GULF OF
MEXICO

AZTEC
EMPIRE, 1519

PACIFIC
OCEAN

Introduction

Many different groups lived in ancient Mexico. One group was the Aztecs. They are known for building great temples and killing people for their gods. The Aztecs also invented a calendar, used cactus fibers to make clothes, and made one of the world's first chocolate drinks.

The biggest Aztec city was Tenochtitlan. It was on an island in the middle of Lake Texcoco. The Aztecs lived in this city from about 1325 to 1521. The capital of modern Mexico, Mexico City, stands where Tenochtitlan once was. Many Aztec ruins lie beneath Mexico City's streets. These traces of the Aztecs tell us a lot about life in their ancient city.

CHAPTER ONE

Living in Tenochtitlan

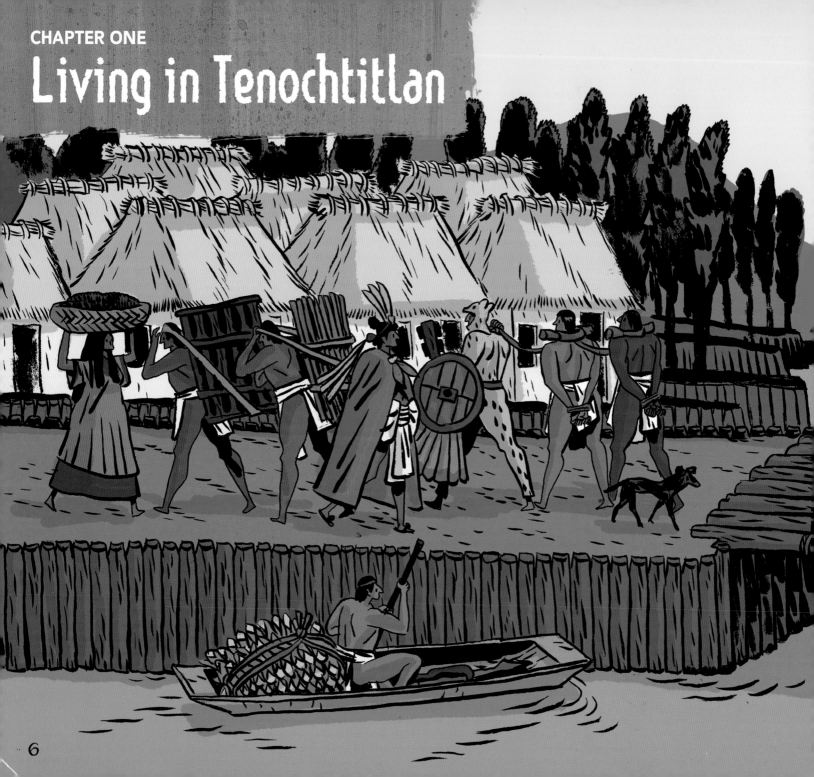

Tenochtitlan was a large city. More than two hundred thousand people lived there. But life was not the same for all people. The Aztecs were divided into three classes, or groups. The top group was the nobles. They had the best clothing and houses.

Commoners made up the next group. They lived in neighborhoods of about one hundred families. Men worked as farmers or traders. Women took care of the house, cooked food, and raised children. Women also made cloth.

Slaves were the lowest group. The Aztecs captured many slaves in wars. Most slaves worked for the nobles.

The Aztecs called themselves Mexica.

7

People of different classes wore different clothing. But the basics were the same for everyone. Men wore a cloth around the waist and a cloak. Women often wore a skirt and a blouse. Some people used clothing to bet on the popular game *tlachtli*.

The Aztecs had laws about what people could wear. A person wearing the wrong clothing could be killed! Nobles dressed in brightly colored cotton clothes. They wore necklaces, earrings, and other jewelry.

Common people and slaves wore plainer clothing. They made cloth for their clothes from cactus fibers. By law, their clothing could not be brightly colored. And they couldn't wear gold jewelry.

In the game *tlachtli*, two teams competed to put a ball through a small ring (right). Players had to hit the ball with their legs, hips, and elbows.

For Aztecs, the most important food was maize, or corn. The Aztecs ground maize into flour. They used the flour to make tortillas, a type of flat bread. The Aztecs also made a chocolate drink. They poured the liquid from one container to another to make it foamy. Only the nobles could drink it.

Other Aztec foods included popcorn, peanuts, fruits, and vegetables. People ate fish and waterbirds from the lake. The Aztecs may even have raised dogs as food.

Most Aztecs ate two meals a day— one in the morning and one in the evening.

Aztec parents raised their children to be well behaved. They punished children who did not obey. Parents taught their children the skills they needed to make a living. By the age of seven, boys could catch fish in nets. Girls could spin cotton into thread.

Children also went to school. The nobles and common people had separate schools. Girls and boys went to different schools too. Girls studied subjects such as music and dance. Boys also learned music and dance. But most of their lessons were about war.

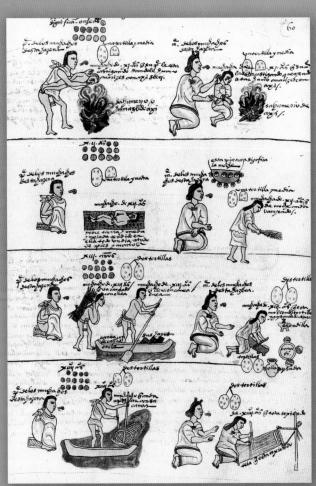

This is a page from a book created in about 1500. The top four images show how bad children were punished. The bottom four images show children helping with important work, such as harvesting crops, rolling tortillas, catching fish, and weaving.

The idea of the cartoon speech bubble may have come from the Aztecs. Their drawings of people include small blue glyphs. These symbols show that someone is speaking.

War was a big part of Aztec life. The Aztecs had no permanent army. Instead, every man had to fight when city leaders needed him.

The Aztecs fought with spears and swords. They made these weapons from sharpened stones attached to pieces of wood. Warriors wore thick cotton padding for armor.

Warriors tried to capture many enemy soldiers in battle. A warrior became more important by capturing many enemy soldiers. Some captives became slaves. The Aztecs killed other captives to please their gods.

In battle, Aztecs used shields to protect themselves. This shield is decorated with feathers and sheets of gold.

Great warriors dressed as eagles, jaguars, or other animals when they went off to fight.

15

CHAPTER TWO

Religion

Religion was important for all Aztecs. The Aztecs believed in about two hundred gods. They built temples to worship these gods.

The biggest temple was the Great Temple. This temple stood in the middle of Tenochtitlan. It was shaped like a pyramid. It had two parts at the top. One side was for Huitzilopochtli, the sun god. The other was for Tlaloc, the rain god.

These steps are the remains of the Great Temple.

The Great Temple was about 200 feet (60 meters) tall.

The Aztecs celebrated eighteen festivals each year. Different festivals were for different gods. A festival in early summer was called the Little Feast of the Lords. During this time, the Aztecs decorated the city with flowers. Salt makers danced and sang. The nobles held feasts and invited the commoners. Sacrifices also took place at festivals.

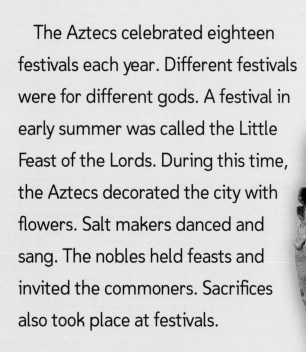

This is a statue of Xochipilli, the god of flowers and dancing.

The Little Feast of the Lords celebrated two gods. One was the god of flowers and dancing. The other was the goddess of salt.

To please their gods, the Aztecs sacrificed many people. Priests were in charge of the sacrifices. Most of the people killed were captured warriors or slaves. But sometimes the Aztecs killed children. People thought killing children for Tlaloc would bring rain.

One god, Quetzalcoatl, was different. He had the body of a snake and the wings of a bird. He did not want human sacrifices. Instead, the Aztecs offered him birds, snakes, and butterflies.

The Aztecs believed they had to make sacrifices. They thought the sun needed blood. Without blood, the sun might stop shining. The world might end.

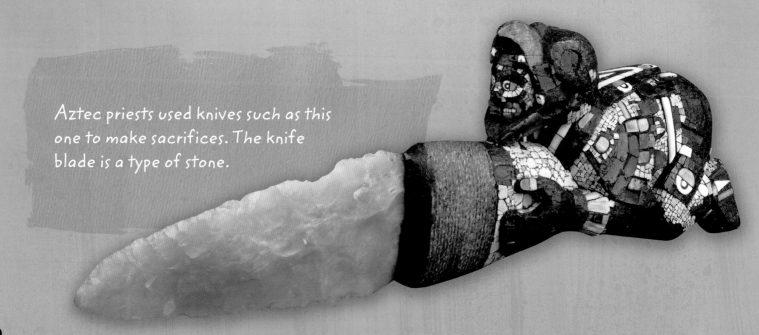

Aztec priests used knives such as this one to make sacrifices. The knife blade is a type of stone.

Priests rubbed ashes on their skin. Most priests were nobles.

CHAPTER THREE

Inside the City

Tenochtitlan was the largest city in ancient Mexico. It had wide streets. The neighborhoods were clean and organized. Every part of Tenochtitlan was carefully planned.

A huge market stood at one end of the city. As many as sixty thousand people may have traded there each day. Traders brought goods from far away. People bought and sold food, pottery, cloth, jewelry, slaves, and more.

The Aztecs used cacao beans (left) as money. They also used the beans to make chocolate. One bean could buy one large tomato. A small rabbit cost thirty beans.

Common people in Tenochtitlan lived in small houses. The walls were made of mud brick. Leaves covered the roofs.

Families did not own much. They had a stone to grind corn. They used griddles for cooking tortillas and pots for beans and other foods. People ate from clay plates and bowls.

Many people also had clay figures of gods and temples. People used the figures to worship at home.

Common people could not build a house with two levels. A person who disobeyed this law could be killed.

25

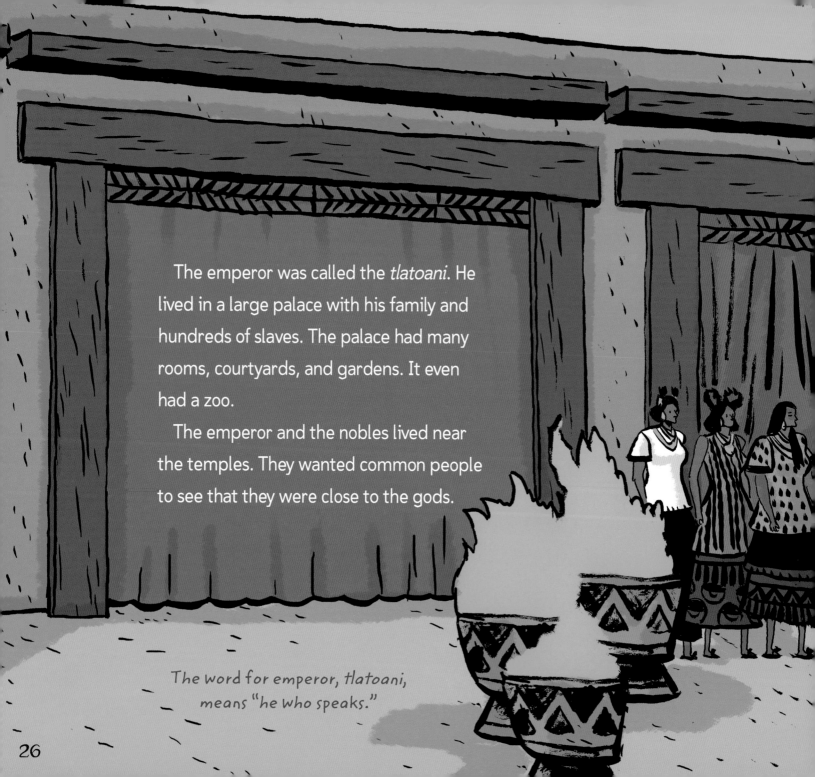

The emperor was called the *tlatoani*. He lived in a large palace with his family and hundreds of slaves. The palace had many rooms, courtyards, and gardens. It even had a zoo.

The emperor and the nobles lived near the temples. They wanted common people to see that they were close to the gods.

The word for emperor, *tlatoani*, means "he who speaks."

CHAPTER FOUR

Ideas and Inventions

The Aztecs thought of many new ideas. They had scientists, scholars, poets, and artists. They studied the movements of the sun and moon. They built a civilization unlike any that came before or after.

Aztec writings tell us a lot about their culture. The Aztecs wrote with pictographs. These pictures and symbols stand for words. The Aztecs created printed works called codices. These tell us about events, government records, laws, and much more.

Aztec books could be unfolded. This book is 13 feet (3.8 m) long when all the pages are spread out.

The Aztecs made paper from the bark of fig trees. First, they pulled off large sheets of bark. Then they soaked them in water, dried them, boiled them, and used stones to pound them into finished flat sheets.

The Aztecs used two calendars. The first kept track of religious festivals. It included just 260 days. The second calendar was 365 days. It had eighteen months of twenty days, plus five extra days. The five extra days came at the end of the year. The Aztecs thought these days were unlucky.

Once every fifty-two years, the two calendars started on the same day. Aztecs believed the world could end on that day. They marked the day with the New Fire Ceremony. People put out their cooking fires. The city was dark. Then priests sacrificed a man and started a new fire at the top of the city's highest hill.

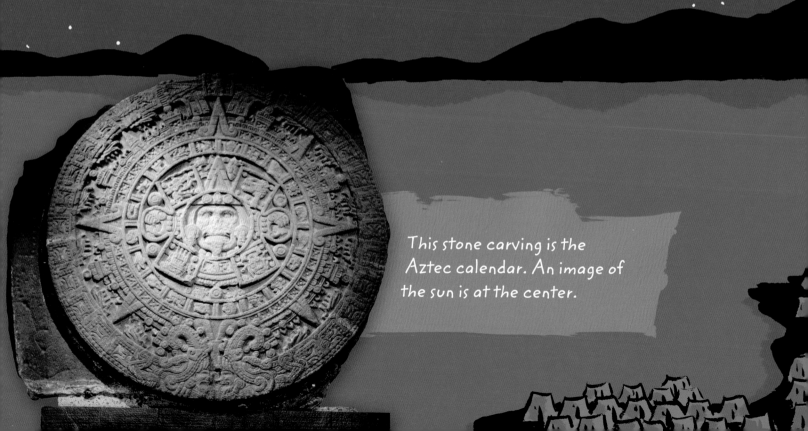

This stone carving is the Aztec calendar. An image of the sun is at the center.

Runners brought the new fire to all the temples and homes in the city.

Aztec inventions helped many people. Healers used herbs to cure sickness. The Aztecs also built aqueducts to bring freshwater into the city. Aqueducts are structures that carry water long distances.

The Aztecs were great farmers. Their *chinampa* farms helped feed the city. These "floating farms" were on islands in Lake Texcoco. Farmers piled up mud from the bottom of the lake to form the islands. With rich soil and plenty of water, the crops grew quickly.

Farmers traveled between fields in small boats.

33

CHAPTER FIVE

Ruling the Empire

Aztec emperors often led their people into wars. They fought with other leaders so they could control more land and more people. They also fought to take captives.

Itzcoatl ruled from 1427 to 1440. He formed a partnership with two nearby cities, Texcoco and Tlacopan. This Triple Alliance created the Aztec Empire. Itzcoatl and his alliance fought wars with many nearby peoples to make the empire larger.

Aztec warriors did not usually kill their enemies when they fought. Instead, they tried to take many captives.

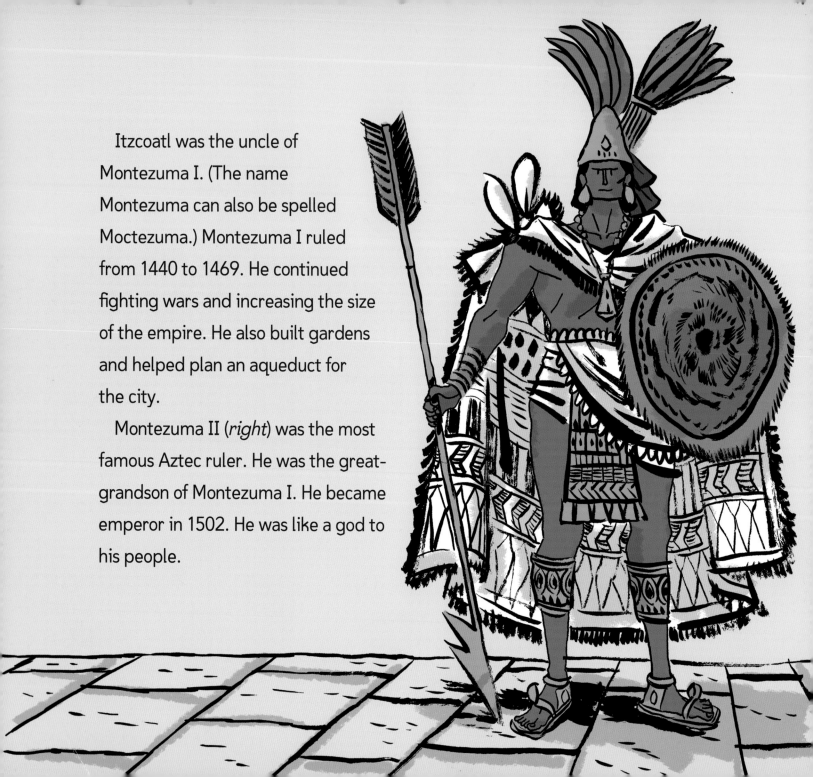

Itzcoatl was the uncle of Montezuma I. (The name Montezuma can also be spelled Moctezuma.) Montezuma I ruled from 1440 to 1469. He continued fighting wars and increasing the size of the empire. He also built gardens and helped plan an aqueduct for the city.

Montezuma II (*right*) was the most famous Aztec ruler. He was the great-grandson of Montezuma I. He became emperor in 1502. He was like a god to his people.

Nobles carried Montezuma II through the city on a special chair with handles.

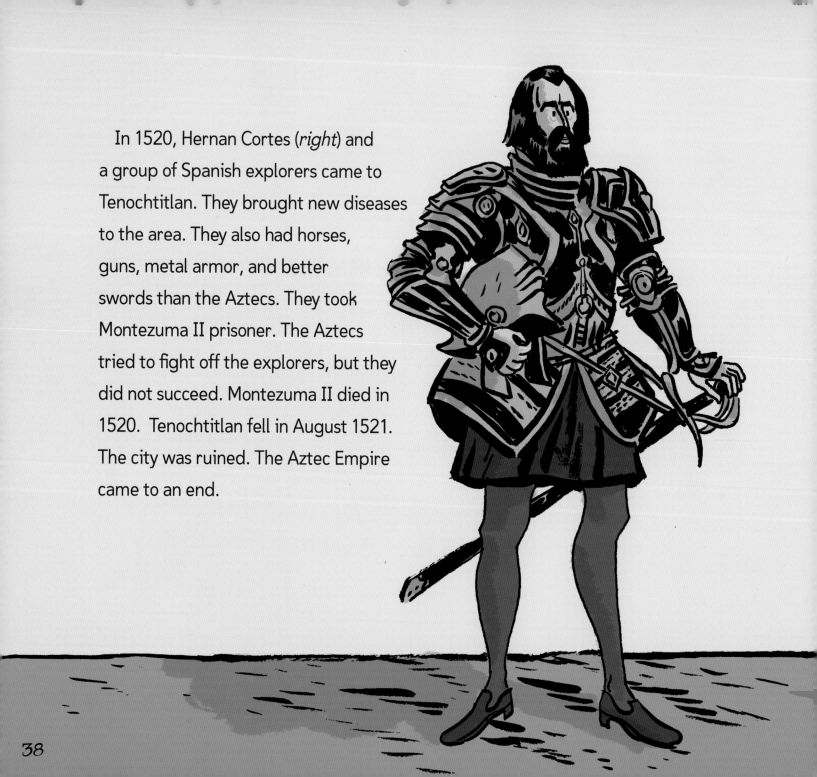

In 1520, Hernan Cortes (*right*) and a group of Spanish explorers came to Tenochtitlan. They brought new diseases to the area. They also had horses, guns, metal armor, and better swords than the Aztecs. They took Montezuma II prisoner. The Aztecs tried to fight off the explorers, but they did not succeed. Montezuma II died in 1520. Tenochtitlan fell in August 1521. The city was ruined. The Aztec Empire came to an end.

Before the Aztecs fought the Spanish, many Aztec warriors were weakened or killed by smallpox. Spanish explorers brought this disease to the Americas.

CHAPTER SIX

Echoes of the Aztecs

Much of the Aztecs' past is a mystery. The Spanish destroyed and burned buildings, books, and other symbols of the Aztec culture. The people mixed with the Spanish. The Spanish brought Christian beliefs to the region. Aztec culture slowly faded.

Some Aztecs saw that their way of life was ending. One man wrote a poem as he watched Tenochtitlan fall. Part of the poem reads:

Our city is lost and dead.
The shields of our warriors were its defense,
but they could not save it.

People related to the Aztecs are called the Nahua. The name comes from the Aztec language, Nahuatl.

Mexico has changed a lot since Aztec times. People drained the water from Lake Texcoco. Mexico City fills the valley where Tenochtitlan once stood. The modern city is built upon the ruins of the ancient city. Many Aztec objects still rest beneath its streets.

Traces of the Aztec people also remain. Almost all Mexicans have some Aztec heritage. The Aztec language, Nahuatl, has blended with Spanish. Some Aztec words have even worked their way into English. Tomato, chili, and tamale are just a few such words.

Scientists who study ancient cultures dig to find Aztec ruins. The ruins help us imagine the lives of the Aztecs long ago. They also remind us of a fascinating culture that existed long before Europeans came to the Americas.

These scientists are uncovering Aztec ruins that are buried under Mexico City.

Modern Mexico City has a population of more than 8 million people.

TIMELINE

1325 The Aztecs settle near Lake Texcoco and found the city of Tenochtitlan.

1428 Itzcoatl begins to build the Aztec Empire by forming the Triple Alliance.

1440 Itzcoatl dies. Montezuma I takes over as emperor.

1446–1455 A food shortage weakens the empire.

1469 Montezuma I dies.

1487 The emperor Ahuitzotl dedicates the Great Temple.

1500 A flood destroys much of Tenochtitlan.

1502 Montezuma II becomes emperor.

1519 Spanish explorers, led by Cortes, arrive in Mexico.

1520 Cortes visits Montezuma II in Tenochtitlan.

1520 Montezuma II dies.

1521 Tenochtitlan falls to Cortes, and the Aztec Empire falls along with it.

1790s Scientists dig beneath Mexico City and find many Aztec ruins.

1913 Workers tearing down a building in Mexico City uncover a corner of the Great Temple.

1987 The Museum of the Great Temple opens to display the objects found at the site of the Great Temple.

PRONUNCIATION GUIDE

aqueducts (AH-kwuh-ducks)

chinampa (chee-NAM-pah)

codices (KOH-dih-seez)

Huitzilopochtli (weet-sih-loh-POHCH-tli)

Itzcoatl (eets-koh-AT-tl)

Mexica (meh-SHEE-kah)

Montezuma (mahn-tuh-ZOO-muh)

Nahua (NAH-wah)

Nahuatl (NAH-waht-uhl)

Quetzalcoatl (ket-zahl-koh-WAH-tl)

Tenochtitlan (tay-NOHTCH-teet-LAHN)

Texcoco (tesh-KOH-koh)

tlachtli (TLACH-tlee)

Tlaloc (tlah-LOHK)

tlatoani (tlah-toh-AH-nee)

tortillas (tor-TEE-uhz)

Xochipilli (sho-chee-PEE-lee)

GLOSSARY

alliance: an agreement to work together

aqueducts: man-made structures that carry water long distances

captives: enemy soldiers captured in battle

chinampa: a floating farm made from lake mud piled above the surface of Lake Texcoco

codices: Aztec books, written in pictographs

empire: an area ruled by one emperor

herbs: plants used in cooking or medicine

maize: another word for corn. Maize was the main food the Aztecs ate.

Nahuatl: the language of the Aztecs

pictograph: a form of writing that uses pictures instead of letters and numbers

sacrifice: an offering to a god. The Aztecs believed in offering the lives of human beings to keep their gods happy.

smallpox: a disease that Spanish explorers brought to the Americas. It killed many Aztecs and other native peoples.

tlatoani: an Aztec emperor

tortillas: flat breads made from ground corn

FURTHER READING

Baquedano, Elizabeth. *Aztec, Inca & Maya*. New York: DK Pub., 2005.
This book covers three of the largest empires of the ancient Americas. It describes the history, beliefs, rituals, and daily life of the Aztec, Inca, and Maya people.

Dawson, Imogen. *Clothes and Crafts in Aztec Times*. Milwaukee: Gareth Stevens, 2000.
Dawson's simple text discusses the basic Aztec culture, with a focus on arts, crafts, clothing, and jewelry.

Jolley, Dan. *The Smoking Mountain: The Story of Popocatépetl and Iztaccíhuatl*. Minneapolis: Graphic Universe, 2009.
This graphic novel presents an Aztec legend in which a great warrior falls in love with the emperor's daughter.

MacDonald, Fiona. *How to Be an Aztec Warrior*. Washington, DC: National Geographic, 2005.
Find out about the duties of an Aztec warrior and what life—and battle—was like for warriors.

Steele, Phillip. *The Aztec News*. Milwaukee: Gareth Stevens, 2001.
This fun book is set up in the style of a newspaper published by the ancient Aztecs. Articles in the newspaper cover everything from sports in the Aztec world to the coming of the Spanish.

Streissguth, Tom. *Mexico*. Minneapolis: Lerner Publications Company, 2008.
Colorful photographs and simple text provide an introduction to modern-day Mexico.

WEBSITES

The Aztec Calendar
http://www.azteccalendar.com
This site offers a closer look at how Aztec calendars worked.

Aztec Gods and Goddesses
http://www.crystalinks.com/aztecgods.html
Check out a list of major Aztec gods, along with brief descriptions and images.

Aztecs at Mexicolore
http://www.mexicolore.co.uk/index.php?one=azt
This website contains many questions from students. Experts provide the answers. The site also includes many photos and illustrations.

Nahuatl Words in Mexican Spanish Vocabulary
http://www.azteca.net/aztec/nahuatl/nahuawds.html
Learn Nahuatl words, and see both Mexican Spanish and English translations.

Royal Academy of Arts—The Aztecs
http://www.aztecs.org.uk
The Royal Academy of Arts' site on the Aztecs includes history as well as images of artwork and artifacts of the ancient Aztecs.

The Zocalo (Differentworld.com)
http://www.differentworld.com/mexico/areas/mexico-city/guide-zocalo.htm
This travel guide to modern Mexico City includes photographs and visiting tips about Aztec ruins and other sites of interest.

INDEX

PHOTO ACKNOWLEDGMENTS

The images in this book are used with the permission of: © Philadelphia Museum of Art/CORBIS, p. 8; The Art Archive/Bodleian Library Oxford, p. 12; © SuperStock, Inc./SuperStock, pp. 14, 30; © Dyana/Alamy, p. 16; © Scala/Art Resource, NY, p. 18; © British Museum/Art Resource, NY, p. 20; © iStockphoto.com/Howard Sandler, p. 22; © Werner FormanArt Resource, NY, p. 28; © F.CASTILLO/AFP/Getty Images, p. 42.

About the Illustrations

Samuel Hiti, who has a background in comic-book art, rendered the illustrations for the Life in Ancient Civilizations series using brush, ink, and computer. Hiti researched each civilization to develop distinct color palettes for these books and create his interpretations of life in these cultures.

For Jen —MD

Millbrook Press
A division of Lerner Publishing Group, Inc.
241 First Avenue North
Minneapolis, MN 55401 U.S.A.

Website address: www.lernerbooks.com

Library of Congress Cataloging-in-Publication Data

Doeden, Matt.
      The Aztecs : life in Tenochtitlan / by Matt Doeden ; illustrated by Samuel Hiti.
                  p.   cm. — (Life in ancient civilizations)
            Includes index.
            ISBN: 978-0-8225-8684-5 (lib. bdg. : alk. paper)
            1. Aztecs—History—Juvenile literature. 2. Aztecs—Social life and customs—Juvenile literature.
      [1. Aztecs—History. 2. Aztecs—Social life and customs.] I. Hiti, Samuel. II. Title.
      F1219.73.D64 2010
      972'.501—dc22   2008047787

Manufactured in the United States of America
1 2 3 4 5 6 – DP – 15 14 13 12 11 10